SAM
HOUSTON

I AM HOUSTON

bright sky press
HOUSTON, TEXAS

2365 Rice Boulevard, Suite 202,
Houston, Texas 77005

10   9   8   7   6   5   4   3   2   1
Library of Congress Cataloging-in Publication Data

Wade, Mary Dodson.
Sam Houston : I am Houston / by Mary Dodson Wade.
p. cm. -- (Texas heroes for young readers ; 2)
ISBN 978-1-933979-37-3 (hardcover : alk. paper)
1. Houston, Sam, 1793-1863--Juvenile literature. 2. Governors--Texas--Biography--Juvenile literature. 3. Legislators--United States--Biography--Juvenile literature. 4. United States. Congress.
Senate--Biography--Juvenile literature. 5. Soldiers--Texas--Biography--Juvenile literature.
6. Texas--History--To 1846--Juvenile literature. I. Title. II. Series.

F390.H84W334 2009
976.4'04092--dc22
[B]   2009008162

Book and cover design by Cregan Design
Illustrations by Pat Finney
Printed in China through Asia Pacific Offset

SAM
HOUSTON
I AM HOUSTON

MARY DODSON WADE

ILLUSTRATIONS BY

PAT FINNEY

bright sky press
HOUSTON, TEXAS

TABLE OF CONTENTS

CHAPTER 1

....

Willful Boy

Captain Samuel Houston urged his horse homeward to Timber Ridge Plantation in Rockbridge County, Virginia. Just a few days after he reached the handsome two-story house he had inherited from his father, another son arrived. To this fifth son, born March 2, 1793, Captain Houston gave his own name.

In the next few years, another son and three daughters joined young Sam Houston and his brothers. Their father, an army officer, was gone for long periods of time. Elizabeth Paxton Houston cared for the children and managed the plantation.

Sam grew tall for his age. School did not appeal to him, but Elizabeth Houston encouraged his love of reading. He devoured books on history and geography that he found in his father's library.

By the time Sam was fourteen, however, his father had died, and their money was gone. Elizabeth Houston sold Timber Ridge. She packed her nine children and their belongings into two wagons and set out down the Shenandoah Valley. The 300-mile trip ended in Blount County, Tennessee, about ten miles south of Maryville. The older Houston boys cleared land, built a cabin, and planted a tobacco crop.

Sam, a tall, good-looking lad with wavy brown hair and piercing blue-gray eyes, was not interested in farm work. He enrolled at Porter Academy where he discovered the *Iliad*. This book about Greek heroes inspired him to want to learn Greek. The teacher refused to teach him, and Sam walked out.

His older brothers sent him to work in a dry goods store. Being in the store all day seemed worse than being in school where he could not learn what he wanted to know. Sam disappeared into the forest.

After weeks of searching, his brothers found him ninety miles away, living with Cherokee Indians on

Hiwasee Creek. When his brothers came to get him, Sam balked. He "preferred measuring deer tracks, to tape." His brothers left him there.

Chief Oo-loo-te-ka was head of about 300 peaceful Cherokee. He considered Sam his son and gave him the Indian name Co-lon-neh. It meant *Raven*. Life with the Cherokee suited Sam perfectly. He had books. He read the *Iliad* so many times that he could quote long parts of it. Best of all, no one told him what to do.

Sam mastered Cherokee games and skills. He began to think as they did. He adopted the custom of talking about himself as if he were someone else. He never said "I" but called his own name instead. When he was old, Sam Houston fondly remembered those days. "Houston has since seen nearly all there is in life to live for, and yet… there's nothing half so sweet to remember as this sojourn he made among the untutored children of the forest."

After three years, nineteen-year-old Sam went back to Maryville. He needed money. People scoffed when he announced he was going to be a teacher. He had little schooling himself.

The fee for each pupil was eight dollars. This was higher than other teachers charged. And he was specific about how it was to be paid. One-third of his salary was to

be given to him in cash, one-third in corn for his horse, and one-third in bright calico cloth. He wanted new shirts.

It wasn't long before the classroom was completely filled. The teacher stood over six feet tall, his hair hanging in a braid down his back. The future general was happy with his first command.

His signature matched his colorful shirts. He boldly made the letters and then put many swirls and scrolls under them. With the "S" separated from the other letters of his first name, it seemed to say "I am Houston."

CHAPTER 2

....

Brave Soldier

In 1813 the United States was at war with England again. Sam Houston was barely twenty years old. He was in town the day soldiers in white pantaloons and smart waistcoats marched into Maryville looking for volunteers. Local militia volunteers wore homespun outfits, but these soldiers had real uniforms. He stepped forward and picked up the silver dollar off the drum. With that, he became a soldier in the regular army.

As he left, Elizabeth Houston gave her son a gun and slipped a ring on his finger. "While the door of my cottage is open to brave men," she said. "it is eternally shut against cowards."

Houston was a natural leader. In just a few months he became head of an infantry platoon. The American soldiers were ordered by General Andrew Jackson to crush Creek Indians, who had sided with the English troops.

The Creek stronghold was in a great bend of the Tallapoosa River in central Alabama. As Houston led a charge, a barbed arrow struck him in the leg. He ordered a soldier to pull it out. The great effort in removing the arrow left a huge gash in his leg.

General Jackson rode by and ordered the wounded soldier to stay behind the lines, but Houston was not through fighting. When the call came to storm the fortifications, the infantry leader dashed out. No one followed him. A bullet shattered his shoulder, and he stumbled back to safety.

General Jackson noted the young officer's courage, but the army doctors did not bother to treat his wounds. It would be a waste of medicine. They expected him to die before morning.

Houston did not die. Two months after the Battle of Horseshoe Bend, he arrived home. He was so gaunt that his mother recognized him only by his eyes. Doctors later removed the bullet from his shoulder, but the wound never completely healed.

Not long afterwards, because of his knowledge about Indians, Houston got a government appointment as Indian agent. He ordered blankets, got pots for the women, and supplied traps for the hunters.

The Cherokee had signed a treaty saying they would move west to territory reserved for them. Houston encouraged his friends to go, but the Cherokee believed the West was a place of destruction and death. Proof of this seemed to come when one of their chiefs returned from there with the report that his people were starving.

Houston accompanied the chief to Washington to ask for food and supplies the government had promised. When Secretary of War John C. Calhoun saw Houston dressed as a Cherokee, he was outraged. He sternly reprimanded the young lieutenant for being out of uniform.

Houston did not care what the Secretary of War thought of his clothes, but he was furious when he was accused of stealing from the Indians. He exposed the guilty persons, but no one was punished. Houston wrote an angry letter resigning from the army.

CHAPTER 3

Success in Tennessee

At the age of twenty-five, Sam Houston moved to Nashville, Tennessee, to study law. Judge James Trimble, a family friend, took Houston as an apprentice. The judge explained that it would take a year and a half of reading law books to learn enough to be an attorney. Six months later Houston passed the state law examination.

He set up law practice in Lebanon about thirty miles away. A merchant rented him an office for a dollar a month and provided proper clothes to wear. The lawyer in tight breeches, colorful vest, plum-colored coat, and beaver hat caught everyone's attention. Houston joined the local dramatic club. He charmed the ladies with his courteous manners. Men enjoyed debating politics with him.

On his many trips to Nashville, Houston often stopped at the Hermitage, Andrew Jackson's big plantation. The Jacksons treated him like a son. The young lawyer admired the powerful Tennessee politician. He often sent presents to "Aunt Rachel" Jackson. When she died, he led the pallbearers at her funeral.

With Jackson's help, Houston became head of the Tennessee state militia. Before long, his success as a trial lawyer led to the job of state attorney general. Then, in 1823, he was elected congressman from Tennessee. This time, he walked the streets of Washington dressed as a fashionable gentleman. In Congress, his long, dramatic speeches were filled with stories from the books he had read.

Four years later, the dashing congressman left Washington to become governor of Tennessee. He was so popular that there was even talk of his running for president. It seemed just one more happy event when he married young Eliza Allen on January 29, 1829. Her prominent family would be a great help for anyone in public office. And what a prize for her to be married to the popular thirty-five-year-old governor!

But the marriage did not last. Less than three months later, Eliza left her husband and returned to her father's house. Houston's enemies seized the scandal to spread ugly rumors that he had wronged Eliza. His friends urged him to speak out and defend himself, but he sealed his lips. He dared anyone to speak ill of Eliza. To his death, he kept that silence. "It is no part of the conduct of a… generous man to take up arms against a woman," he said. "If my character cannot stand the shock, let me lose it."

It was not his character, however, that suffered. It was his career. On April 16, 1829, he sat in his room near the Tennessee capitol building. Dipping the feather pen, he struggled with the words, crossing them out again and again. Finally, he completed the long letter. "It has become my duty to resign the office of Chief Magistrate of the State."

CHAPTER 4

The Raven Returns

A week later, Houston boarded a steamer to leave Tennessee. A few miles downstream, an eagle soared overhead with a scream. Then it disappeared into the sunset. It was a symbol the Raven understood. "I knew that a great…destiny awaited me in the West."

Before many days he was again with the Cherokee. They had moved to their new home among the cottonwood trees on the Arkansas River in the territory reserved for Indian tribes (Oklahoma). Chief Oo-loo-te-ka welcomed him. "My son, eleven winters have passed since we met…I heard that you were a great chief among your people…The Great Spirit has sent you to us to give us

counsel and take trouble away from us…My people are yours—rest with us."

The Raven slipped easily into Cherokee life. He attended councils dressed in a beaded white-doeskin shirt and long yellow leggings. On his head he wore a colorful turban. He became spokesman for a number of other tribes, and the Cherokee declared him to be their full-blood brother.

A year after leaving Tennessee, Houston returned to Washington wearing a colorful Cherokee hunting shirt and buckskin pants. Andrew Jackson was now president. Houston told him about the problems the tribes were having. Jackson listened and removed many of the dishonest Indian agents.

After returning to the Cherokee, Houston built a large house on the Neosho River. He took Tiana Rogers, a Cherokee widow, as his wife. But dark days came for the Raven. For months he did nothing but drink whiskey. He stopped speaking at councils. The Indians gave him a new name—"Big Drunk."

CHAPTER 5

....

To Texas

In the fall of 1831, things changed. Houston received word that his mother was ill. He sped to Tennessee for a last visit with her. The death of this woman he admired stirred him to action.

Soon he was back in Washington to help his Indian friends. He wore a buckskin coat with beaver collar, the gift of an Indian chief. A hunting knife hung at his belt, and he carried a cane that he had carved when he and the Cherokee delegation had stopped at the Hermitage.

While he was in Washington, Congressman William Stanbery of Ohio accused him of dishonesty in dealing with the Indians. Raging with anger, Houston challenged the congressman to a duel. Stanbery refused, but started carrying a gun.

One day the two large men met on the street. Houston began to beat Stanbery with his cane. The congressman pulled out his gun, but it failed to fire. Houston continued his attack, tearing Stanbery's shirt, fracturing his left hand, and giving Stanbery a concussion.

The brawl was the talk of Washington. Stanbery insisted that Houston be tried by the House of Representatives for attacking one of its members. President Jackson sent for his favorite. When Houston arrived in his usual Cherokee outfit, Jackson flung money at him and told him to get some new clothes. Houston, always conscious of how he looked, set off to the tailor to be measured for a coat and trousers of the finest material.

On the day of the trial, every seat in Congress was filled. Francis Scott Key, author of "The Star-Spangled Banner," acted as Houston's lawyer. After the charge was read, Key presented the defense.

Houston insisted that he speak as well. Dressed in a stylish dark waistcoat that reached his knees, matching trousers, and white satin vest, he lifted his voice in an impassioned speech. He insisted that Congress

had no right to bring charges against a private citizen. Cheers erupted when he finished, but he was found guilty anyway.

The Speaker of the House, however, made short work of the punishment. He praised Houston, then announced that the verdict required him to censure Houston. By reading the verdict, he said, he had done that. Houston never paid the $500 fine.

The whole affair brought him back into politics. He gave Tiana the big house on the Neosho River and never returned to live with the Cherokee.

As Andrew Jackson's representative, Houston crossed the Red River into Texas in early December 1832. Jackson, like many Americans, believed Texas had been part of the Louisiana Purchase and that it should be American territory, not Mexican.

Officially, Houston was there to survey the Indian situation. His passport from the United States requested safe passage among all Indian tribes for "General Samuel Houston, a Citizen of the United States, Thirty-eight years of age, Six feet, two inches in stature, brown hair and light complexion."

Traveling through east Texas, he met Cherokee Chief Duwali, often called Chief Bowles or Bowl. Houston traveled on to Nacogdoches and then to San Felipe de Austin, headquarters for Stephen F. Austin's colony. The empresario who had brought American settlers to Texas was not in town. Houston ate Christmas dinner with James Bowie.

Afterwards, the two rode to San Antonio de Béxar, the center of Mexican government for Texas. Bowie introduced Houston to his father-in-law, Vice-Governor Don Juan Veramendi. Houston charmed the vice-governor's wife.

Returning to Louisiana, Houston sent Jackson a report saying Texas citizens favored joining the United States twenty to one. Houston felt sure they would form a state government, and he expected to attend the convention. His 500-mile trip convinced him this area was the finest on the globe. "I may make Texas my abiding place."

CHAPTER 6

Drafting Texas Independence

Sam Houston was a delegate to the 1833 convention meeting in San Felipe de Austin. The delegates adopted a constitution separating Texas from the Mexican state of Coahuila. When Stephen Austin left to present the document to the Mexican government, Houston returned to Nacogdoches.

He established a successful law practice in a log building off the town square. He entered into the town's social life and won the hearts of the ladies. Seventeen-year-old Anna Raguet, a well-educated young woman, began teaching Spanish to the fashionable bachelor, and he began to court her.

Houston lived with *Alcalde* (Mayor) Adolphus Sterne. Because Mexico required all settlers to become Catholics, Houston was baptized in the Sterne home. Eva Rosine Sterne acted as his godmother. Ever afterwards, he referred to her as "Madre Mio" and showered her with presents.

Austin, meanwhile, had been imprisoned in Mexico. The government there considered the petition for separate Texas statehood to be treason. Texans, believing they would never get what they wanted, began a clamor for independence from Mexico. When Austin was finally released two years later, he acknowledged that war with Mexico was inevitable.

Almost immediately, Mexican dictator Antonio López de Santa Anna sent his brother-in-law, General Martín Perfecto Cós, to San Antonio to put down the rebellion. Texans forced Cós to surrender and retreat. This sent Santa Anna into a rage.

With war looming, Sam Houston was named commander-in-chief of the Texas army. Anna Raguet tied a woven silk sash on Houston's sword and sent him off. But no one expected Mexican troops to march north during the winter.

Houston sent Bowie to San Antonio with orders

to abandon fortifications there. Bowie did not carry out those instructions. When the Mexican army suddenly appeared outside San Antonio on February 23, 1836, the city's defenders hurried inside the old Alamo mission. General Santa Anna demanded their complete surrender.

While those inside the Alamo waited for help, delegates in Washington-on-the-Brazos worked in a cold, unfinished building to complete the Texas Declaration of Independence. On March 2, 1836, Houston placed his bold signature on the document. He celebrated his forty-third birthday by sending "Madre Mio" a beautiful pair of two-inch-long earrings. He asked her to wear them every year to honor his birthday and that of Texas.

CHAPTER 7

Hero of San Jacinto

While the Texans were trying to complete a constitution for their new republic, a desperate letter arrived from the Alamo commander. William Barret Travis pleaded, "I am besieged by a thousand or more Mexicans under Santa Anna. *I shall never surrender or retreat.* Come to our aid...VICTORY OR DEATH!"

Convention delegates raced for the door, but cooler heads called them back to finish the work of organizing a government. General Houston set out for Gonzales, a hundred miles away. He arrived on March 11 and found nearly 400 men gathered and ready to fight. They had just formed into army units when two Tejano riders raced into town with news that the Alamo had fallen.

Houston sent scout Erastus (Deaf) Smith to check the story. Smith soon returned with Susannah Dickenson, her little girl Angelina, and William Travis' servant Joe. They confirmed the dreadful story. Travis, Bowie, David Crockett and all the other Alamo defenders had died on March 6. Santa Anna had sent these three to carry a warning to the rest of Texas.

Houston ordered the destruction of everything in Gonzales that could not be carried. Terrified citizens fled the town with the departing soldiers. They had not gone far when Houston sent fifty men back to get a blind widow and her children who had been left behind.

Houston retreated to the Guadalupe River and sent word for Goliad commander James Fannin to meet him there with his 500 soldiers. Fannin never got to the Guadalupe. His army had been captured following their defeat at the Battle of Coleto Creek. Only a few survivors escaped to tell of the mass execution of the Goliad prisoners.

The only army Houston had now was the one with him. And some of these troops were leaving to take care of their families as citizens raced to safety in Louisiana.

Houston ordered retreat to the Colorado River. His

untrained recruits were not ready to face the professional Mexican army. As the rain fell, weary soldiers grumbled about their cowardly leader who kept retreating. Houston talked to no one. *"If I err, the blame is mine,"* he wrote Secretary of War Thomas Rusk.

Temporary Texas president David Burnet and the rest of the government were fleeing as well. Burnet sent Houston a scathing letter. "Sir: The enemy are laughing you to scorn. You must fight."

Houston pushed his soldiers through the mud until they reached the Brazos River across from the plantation of Jared Groce. The wealthiest man in the colony provided food for the men and their horses. He supplied lead for bullets and turned his house into a hospital for those who were ill.

For two weeks Houston drilled his soldiers. Then the steamboat *Yellowstone* was pressed into service to ferry the men across the flooded river. Still there was no order to stand and fight. The weary trek began again with citizens in tow.

Several miles southeast they reached a fork in the road. One way led to safety in the United States. The other road led to Harrisburg where they would surely meet the Mexican army. Rain-soaked soldiers, eager to fight, wheeled toward Harrisburg.

Pamelia Mann had no intention of meeting Mexicans. She demanded the return of her oxen that were pulling two cannon. Although General Houston protested, she cut them loose and drove the oxen away. The wagon master followed her. Houston warned him, "That woman will fight." The wagon master returned that evening with a torn shirt, but without the oxen.

Santa Anna had ignored the little Texas army as he raced after fleeing government officials. Leaving a thousand troops at Fort Bend on the west bank of the Brazos, he took 500 soldiers to Harrisburg. He barely missed the Texas officials and started after them.

By great luck, Deaf Smith intercepted a Mexican courier with William Travis' saddlebags. Messages inside showed that Santa Anna was near San Jacinto. Houston pushed his men to that area. They hid in the woods, waiting for the Mexican army to return from a march to Galveston Bay.

On April 21, 1836, while the Mexican army rested and watered their horses, Houston mounted Saracen, a magnificent white horse. About 3:30 in the afternoon the Texas commander raised his sword and ordered his troops to charge. Shouts of "Remember the Alamo!

Remember Goliad!" filled the air as the Texans overran the Mexican fortifications.

Juan Seguín's scouts were in the middle of the action. Houston had left them out of the battle plan, but Seguín angrily retorted that they had more to lose than anyone else. The Tejanos rode into battle wearing cardboard in their hatbands to distinguish them.

During the eighteen-minute battle, Houston had two horses shot from under him. His left ankle was shattered. At the end of the chaos, nine Texans were dead, with thirty more wounded. Mexican losses were over 1,300 dead, wounded, or captured.

Houston collapsed and was laid under an oak tree. While a doctor treated his wound, he arranged three magnolia leaves and wrote a note to Anna Raguet in Nacogdoches. "These are laurels I send you from the battlefield of San Jacinto."

CHAPTER 8

President of Texas

General Santa Anna escaped in the confusion of battle. He found a plain blue shirt and put it on over his gold-braided vest. He almost avoided capture. When brought back to camp, his own men gave him away by shouting, *"El Presidente!"* Santa Anna demanded to be taken to Houston. Many wanted Santa Anna executed on the spot, but Houston refused. Texas could bargain better for freedom if the Mexican dictator were alive.

Several days later, Burnet and other officials arrived at the battlefield. Burnet had such contempt for Houston that he refused to allow the wounded general to board his steamer to go to Galveston. The ship's captain, however, would not sail without the hero of San Jacinto. In Galveston, the critically ill general sailed on a private ship to New Orleans for medical treatment.

Two months later he returned. Texans overwhelmingly elected him president of their new republic. At the end of his inaugural address, Houston dramatically laid his sword on the table, reserving the right to use it again should his country need it.

The president of the new Republic of Texas faced huge war debts. Three secretaries took dictation as Houston crafted letters seeking recognition of Texas by other countries. "In the name of the Republic of Texas, Free, Sovereign and Independent...I, Sam Houston, President thereof, send greetings." At the bottom he put the familiar signature.

CHAPTER 9

....

Marrying Margaret Lea

Under the Texas constitution, the president could not hold office two successive terms. Not one to go quietly, Sam Houston dressed in the garb of George Washington and gave a rousing three-hour farewell speech before leaving the office to Mirabeau Lamar.

On a trip to the East in 1838, he stopped to buy horses at the Bledsoe home near Mobile, Alabama. Antoinette Bledsoe's sister, Margaret Moffett Lea, was there for a visit. Houston was captivated by this educated beauty with violet eyes.

For the next two weeks they walked through the gardens, talked and exchanged poetry. He left with

her promise to marry him. When asked why a talented young woman of twenty would marry a man forty-seven years old, Margaret answered simply that he had won her heart.

Houston's divorce from Eliza Allen was final, Tiana Rogers had died of pneumonia, and Anna Raguet would soon marry his friend Robert Irion. Houston returned from his trip with seven fine horses, but the second trip to Alabama bought him the greatest joy. On May 9, 1840, at the Marion, Alabama, home of her brother Henry, Margaret Lea married Sam Houston.

Their first home was at Cedar Point on Galveston Bay. Houston's friends predicted that the marriage wouldn't last six months, but they were wrong. Margaret was deeply religious. Her gentle ways transformed the man known for his hard drinking and rough language.

Texas, on the other hand, was overwhelmed with economic problems. President Mirabeau Lamar had put in place a brilliant plan to provide money to educate Texas children. He had also moved the capital to Austin on the edge of the frontier. His grand scheme to extend the boundaries of Texas, however, emptied the Texas treasury. Most disturbing to Houston, Lamar had forced the removal of the Cherokee from Texas. Chief

Bowl had been killed in the fighting. Houston's angry denunciation praised the Cherokee chief as a better man than his murderers.

The 1842 election put Houston back in office as president. By enforcing a strict budget, he was able to restore value to Texas money. He considered Austin too dangerous for the capital and tried to move the state archives to a safer place. Boarding house owner Angelina Eberly, who would lose business without the lawmakers, sounded the alarm as the wagons drove away. Local citizens forced the return of the documents.

Houston left the archives in Austin and set up his office at Washington-on-the-Brazos. Margaret joined him, and he brought along his talented wife's rosewood piano. They welcomed their first child, Sam Jr., in May 1843.

Just a few months before the birth of his own son, Houston wrote to Lipan Chief Flaco, whose son had died. "My heart is sad. A dark cloud rests upon your nation… The song of birds is silent…Grass shall not grow in the path between us. Thy brother, Sam Houston."

CHAPTER 10

Outspoken Texas Senator

After ten years, the Republic of Texas was near an end. Hearing that Andrew Jackson was dying, Houston raced to Tennessee to tell his friend that Texas was going to be part of the United States. He arrived three hours too late and wept beside the bed of his mentor.

On February 19, 1846, Houston caught the folds of the flag of the republic as it was lowered for the last time. Instead of retiring, though, he left almost immediately for Washington as senator from the twenty-eighth state of the United States.

For the next thirteen years Sam Houston was in Washington for much of the time. The flamboyant figure

sometimes wore a sombrero with a Mexican blanket thrown over his shoulder. At other times he donned a military cap and a short blue cloak with a bright red lining. Among his favorite vests was one made of leopard skin. He wore it "because the scripture says 'a leopard cannot change his spots.'"

On Sundays he went to church. During the sermon, he carved wooden figures that he gave to children. In the afternoon he wrote Margaret long letters about the sermon. Houston missed his family and filled his letters with advice to the ever-increasing children.

Sam Jr. had ordered six brothers, but the next four children were girls—Nannie (Nancy Elizabeth), Maggie (Margaret Lea), Mollie (Mary Willie), and Nettie (Antoinette Power). When a little brother finally arrived, it was rambunctious Andrew Jackson. A few years later William Rogers was born.

Margaret suffered greatly from asthma, but she faithfully answered her husband's letters. The family spent much of the time near Huntsville at Raven Hill. Because it was eleven miles out in the country, they built the Woodland Home in town. A separate log building allowed Houston to work in peace.

Two of the Houston slaves, Joshua and Eliza, had

come with Margaret when she married Houston. Eliza took care of the children. Joshua, known in the community as an expert blacksmith and wheelwright, helped Margaret maintain the properties. When the family traveled, coachman Tom Blue handled the reins of the four horses pulling the big yellow coach.

Jeff Hamilton came to the family one day when Houston was in Huntsville on business. The child was being sold to pay a man's liquor debt. When Houston saw the frightened boy crying on the slave auction block in the noonday sun, he stormed into the store. He told the storekeeper to put the amount on his bill, then bought Jeff some candy. "I have a little boy almost as old as you with whom you can play," he said as they drove home.

The Houstons bought a fourth house in Independence, Texas, a town with fine schools. Margaret's mother and two sisters lived there. Mrs. Lea was a staunch member of the Baptist church.

Margaret's urging about the church finally found its mark. On a chilly November afternoon in 1854, the Reverend Rufus Burleson baptized Sam Houston in Rocky Creek. The Reverend remarked, "Well, General, all your sins have been washed away."

Houston replied, "If that be the case, Lord help

the fish down below." Houston proved his intentions by pledging to pay half the minister's salary.

In Congress, slavery was the central issue. Although Houston owned slaves, he was devoted to keeping the country together. This caused Southern sympathizers to brand him as a traitor because he voted to balance slave and free states. Houston answered that he knew "neither North nor South...only the Union."

In 1857, as slave states threatened to secede from the United States, Houston hastened home to run for governor. He hoped to keep Texas in the Union. That summer he rode 1,500 miles with a salesman in a red buggy with "Warwick's Patent Plow" painted on the side. He gave forty-seven speeches, some lasting four hours, but voters chose the other candidate.

He returned to Washington for his last two years as senator. He tried to get justice for the Indians and complained that West Point graduates couldn't recognize a deer track. He lost many friends with his fight against secession.

More than anything, he longed to be home with his family. His letters to Margaret were signed, "Love to all. Thy devoted, Houston."

CHAPTER 11

....

Uncompromising Texas Governor

During the next race for Texas governor, one speech was enough to get Houston elected. In December 1859 he moved his family into the three-year-old governor's mansion in Austin.

After much wrangling, the Texas senate bought furniture, including a seven-foot bed for the new governor. Sixteen-year-old Sam Jr. attended an academy in Bastrop, and baby William was only a year old. An extra bedroom was created to make room for the rest of the lively Houston children.

Five-year-old mischievous Andrew was allowed to play in the offices in the Capitol. One day he locked the senators in their meeting room. As he ran home, he threw the key into a flower bed. Only the threat of going to jail made him tell where it was.

In the summer of 1860, Temple Lea Houston, their last child, arrived at the governor's mansion. Afterwards, Margaret was so ill that her husband did not leave her side for ten days.

That year at the San Jacinto celebration, friends nominated the sixty-eight-year-old governor for president, but he withdrew his name. As he predicted, Abraham Lincoln won the election. That caused South Carolina to secede, and other southern states followed.

Houston believed the Confederacy would fail. He predicted bloodshed and suffering as a result of secession. The word "traitor" was hurled at him again. Some even dared him to show his face. Houston rented the balcony of the Tremont House in Galveston and gave a stirring speech that silenced the audience.

Sam Jr. ignored his father's advice and joined the Confederate army. The Texas legislature also ignored the governor. They voted for secession and set March 18, 1861, as the date for every state official to swear an oath of loyalty to the Confederacy.

Houston spent a sleepless night pacing upstairs at

the governor's mansion. At daylight he came down and said, "Margaret, I will never do it."

Noon came. When his name was called to take the oath, there was no answer. He was not there. The office of Texas governor was declared vacant, and a new governor named.

Still claiming to be governor, Houston addressed a letter to Texans, "Fellow-Citizens, In the name of your rights and liberties... In the name of the Constitution of Texas... In the name of my own conscience and manhood... I refuse to take this oath."

It was rumored that President Lincoln offered troops to restore him to office. Houston wanted no bloodshed. Margaret hurriedly packed. She and the children climbed into the big yellow coach for the trip to Cedar Point.

Before Houston left the city, he directed Jeff to drive the small buggy to the Treaty Oak. Houston got down and paced off the spreading branches of the huge 400-year-old tree. It was the last of the fourteen Council Oaks where Comanche and Tonkawa Indians had signed treaties.

Even though the old general didn't agree with secession, he reviewed the Confederate troops where Sam Jr. was training. Margaret had sent her son off with a small Bible. The devastating news that he had been killed at the Battle of Shiloh proved to be false. He was, in fact, severely wounded. The Bible had deflected the bullet.

As the war dragged on, money became scarce. The Houstons sold all their homes and rented a steamboat-shaped house in Huntsville. Sitting in his rawhide-bottom chair under a live oak tree, Houston welcomed nearby Alabama and Coushatta Indians. They sought his help because their sons were being forced to join the army.

Houston had dreams of Texas being a republic again, but the dream slowly faded. In April 1863, seventy-year-old Houston set his affairs in order and signed his will in large, somewhat shaky letters.

On July 26, 1863, Margaret and his children gathered beside his bed. As Margaret read psalms from the Bible late in the afternoon, Sam Houston roused a little and spoke his last words, "Texas…Texas…Margaret."

Margaret took from her husband's hand the ring Elizabeth Houston had placed there fifty years before. The children read the word engraved inside—*Honor.*

TIMELINE

AUTHOR'S NOTE

The man who shaped Texas is buried in Oakwood Cemetery in Huntsville. The Woodland Home is on its original site, now the grounds of Sam Houston State University. The steamboat house has been moved there as well. A museum contains Houston family items, including Houston's leopard vest and some of the little wooden objects he carved. Houston's ring is at the San Jacinto Battlefield Museum.

Margaret Houston moved to Independence after her husband's death. She died four years later while nursing yellow fever victims. Fear of spreading the disease forced her burial in the churchyard of the Independence Baptist Church, not beside her husband as she wished.

Sam Jr. recovered and studied medicine. He inherited his father's sword. Nannie Morrow acted as mother to the younger children. Maggie Williams became a fine writer, and Nettie Bringhurst was a poet. Mollie Morrow ran the post office in Abilene, Texas. Andrew attended West Point, organized a troop of Rough Riders, and for years took care of the San Jacinto battleground. He was a strong advocate of prohibition and women's rights. William became an Indian agent. Temple was a successful lawyer with a gift of oratory and a love of flamboyant clothing like his father.

Jeff Hamilton was a special guest during the Texas Centennial in 1936 and had his picture taken under the Treaty Oak. Although acknowledging the horror of slavery, he remembered Sam Houston fondly as the man who shared cookies with him as he drove the small buggy.

The Treaty Oak is located in Austin on Baylor Street, between 5th and 6th streets. Once called the perfect specimen of a tree, it was severely damaged by a deliberate poisoning in 1989. The man who did it went to jail. A genetically identical tree has been planted beside the Treaty Oak.

Eliza lived the rest of her life as a member of the Houston families. She took care of Margaret's small children and her grandchildren. At her request, she was buried in Independence next to Margaret Houston.

Joshua Houston, who like Eliza was about the same age as Margaret, became a leader in Huntsville. He could read and write, and Houston slaves were allowed to keep anything they earned by working for others. After Houston died, Margaret had little money. Joshua rode to Independence with a worn leather bag containing his life savings. He poured out $2,000 in gold and American currency, but she refused the gift. Instead, she urged him to educate his children with the money. Son Joshua Houston Jr. and daughter Minnie Houston studied at Prairie View Normal (Prairie View A&M). Son Samuel Walker Houston attended both Atlanta University and Howard University in Washington D.C. before returning to Huntsville to head a manual training school for freedmen. An elementary school in Huntsville is named for Samuel W. Houston.

Joel Robinson, one of the men who captured Santa Anna, took the exhausted prisoner up on his horse. A grateful Santa Anna gave him the gold-braided vest he was wearing. For many years, young men in Fayette County wore the "Santa Anna vest" on their wedding day.

A fire badly damaged the 150-year-old governor's mansion in 2008. But most of the furnishings, including the Sam Houston bed, survived because they had been removed while the house was being renovated.

For more than 50 years Eva Sterne faithfully followed Houston's request to honor Texas' birthday. She wore the earrings for the last time at the dedication of the present state capitol building in Austin in 1888.

Sam Houston was as colorful as his clothes. Many portraits capture his personality. Elisabet Ney's statue, a copy of the one created for Statuary Hall in Washington, D.C., stands in the state Capitol. A massive statue near Huntsville is visible for miles on Interstate 45.

SOURCES

Sam Houston's imposing personality sparked either great admiration or deep dislike. Books about him reflect differing views. In writing this biography, I found Marshall DeBruhl's *Sword of San Jacinto: A Life of Sam Houston* (New York: Random House, 1993) helpful.

Madge Thornall Roberts, Houston's great-great-granddaughter, published Margaret and Sam's private letters and included many family stories in *Star of Destiny*. The title refers to the star that both could see when they were far apart.

The book by C. E. Lester, identified as an authentic memoir, is really Houston's autobiography.

Quotations in this book keep their original spelling.

"preferred measuring…" C. Edwards Lester, *The Life of Sam Houston; the Only Authentic Memoir of Him Ever Published* (New York: J. C. Derby, 1883), 22.

"Houston has since seen…" Charles Edwards Lester, *Sam Houston and His Republic* (New York: Burgess, Stringer, 1846), 13.

"While the door of my cabin…" Lester, *Life of SH*, 27.

"It is no part…" Lester, *Life of SH*, 46.

"It has become…" Tennessee State Historical Society, Nashville.

"I knew that…" Rufus C. Burleson, *The Life and Writings of Rufus C. Burleson*, (Printed by Georgia J. Burleson, 1901), 552.

"My son,…" Lester, *Life of SH*, 51.

"General Samuel Houston,,," copy in Retired Classification Files, Indian Bureau, Washington, D.C., as quoted in Marquis James, *The Raven* (Austin: University of Texas Press, 1929), 185.

"I may make…" William Carey Crane, *Life and Select Literary Remains of Sam Houston* (Philadelphia: J.B. Lippincott, 1884, 46.

"I am besieged…" William Barret Travis, "To the People of Texas and All Americans in the World," February 24, 1836. Texas State Library.

"If I err,…" Houston to Thomas J. Rusk, March 29, 1836. Sam Houston, *The Writings of Sam Houston*, 1813-1863, edited by Amelia W. Williams and Eugene C. Barker (8 vols. Austin: University of Texas, 1938-1943), I, 385.

"Sir: The enemy are laughing..." Burnet to Houston, April 7, 1836, printed in *Texas Sentinel*, May 17, 1841.

"That woman will fight." Robert Hancock Hunter, *The Narrative of Robert Hancock Hunter*. (Austin: The Encino Press, 1966), 14.

"These are laurels..." Houston to Anna Raguet. April 21, 1836, *Writings*, I, 415.

"In the name..." As quoted in James, 268.

"He won my heart." Crane, 253.

"My heart is sad..." Houston to Flaco, March 28, 1843, Houston family

"because the scripture..." Houston to Margaret, 1856, Madge Thornall Roberts, *Star of Destiny; The Private Life of Sam and Margaret Houston* (Denton: University of North Texas Press, 1993), 267.

"I have a boy..." Jeff Hamilton, *My Master: TheInside Story of Sam Houston and His Times*, as told to Lenoir Hunt (Dallas: Manfred Van Nort & Co., 1940), 9.

"Well, General, all your sins…" and next paragraph. Houston family story. Roberts, 252.

"neither North nor South…" Crane, 202.

"Love to all…" Houston to Margaret Houston, February 28, 1859. Roberts, 404.

"Margaret, I will never…" Houston family story, Roberts, 298.

"Fellow-Citizens…" Sam Houston, *Writings*, VIII, 277.

"Texas…Texas…" quoted in Roberts, 324.

INDEX